PRAISE FOR MANIFESTING WITH ARCHANGEL RAZIEL - UNDERSTAND SIGNIFICANT ENERGY SECRETS OF LAW OF ATTRACTION

"Energy Secrets of the Law of Attraction" - You would think that the title says it all, but on the contrary there is no way to describe the profound insight that lies within this book.
Even to call it a "book," would be a shortcoming. It's not only a book of incredible insight, but also a functioning workbook. Because of this, it transcends just reading words and having an intellectual understanding. It moves you deeper, guiding you into experiencing a spiritual shift.
Everyone is bound to take something different away from it.
No matter what your level of spiritual seeking, from beginner to advanced the information that lies within is a collective universal response to the one "I" source that we all encompass. "

Guitar Monk Mathew Dixon
www.zerolimitsmusic.com

Contents

Introduction	6
How to Use the Book	9
Angelic Wealth Coaching	11
How Can the Manifestation Process be Described on the Chakras Level	14
Universal Laws & Manifestation	20
A little Energetic Background	25
The Chakras	26
Exercise 1. Chakra Mapping Meditation	32
Let's Look at what this Energy Map Tells You	34
The Two Flow	46
Chakras & Manifestation	53
The Root Chakra	57
The Sacral Chakra	62
The Solar Chakra	68
The Heart Chakra	72
The Troat Chakra	78
The Third Eye Chakra	82
The Crown Chakra	86
How To Clear Your Chakras from the Blocks	89
Execise 2. Clearing the Aura with Archangel Raziel	90
Exercise 3. Grounding & Clearing	93
Exercise 4. Chakra Clearing with the Spiral	96
Exercise 5. Become Conscious Creator	100
Final Thoughts	103

MANIFESTING WITH ARCHANGEL RAZIEL series

Understand Significant Energetic Secrets of Law of Attraction

Theresia Valoczy

Manifesting with Archangel Raziel

Copyright © 2018 Theresia Valoczy
All rights reserved.
ISBN-13: 978-1724771476
ISBN-10: 1724771477

Blessings in my life all come from a message that I have received from Archangel Raziel about manifestation. All conversations lead to myself and the ancient angelic wisdom. I feel infinitely grateful for my journey and hope that these message bring a lot of valuable moments into your life too.

INTRODUCTION

I'm very excited, because I can share with you those spiritual secrets, which helped to to create my dream life and to make my wildest, boldest dreams come true.
I can disclose to you the thoughts which helped to manifest everything I would have liked to accomplish in my life.

Surely you are wondering why for some people the Law of Attraction works great, while others do not experience any change.

I admit that years ago I belonged to that second group of people, the ones for whom it did not work. I got stuck on a level and could not advance from there.

Simply put, anything I used - vision boards, visualization – made nothing to happen.
Can you imagine how flustered I was when I saw that it was so simple for others while
I had no results at all.

Then one day, after a total emotional and financial collapse, I regained my spiritual awareness thanks to an Angelic Wake-up-call Message and the big changes in my life began.
From that point, the law of attraction and the science of manifestation became my mission.
I wanted to know everything. I searched for the secrets that changed millions of lives.
I searched for the exercises that facilitate the conscious creation.
I contacted people who were looking for the same thing as me.
I read countless books, I did courses in order to gain a deep insight into the Law of Attraction, as it may be.

I am endlessly grateful to my mentors, who not only gave me knowledge, but they launched the wonderful way of self-realization and helped to look for even deeper information.

Dr Joe Vitale and Dr Steve G Jones, thank you.
During my meditation journey, I was in contact with people who have been widely known and have used Universal Laws, who believed and maintained contact with the Universe, God, the Angels.
During my conversations about the Virtual Mastermind I got a lot of useful information on this subject.

Those that have been omitted from autobiographical books.

During my journey to the Akasha Shrine, Archangel Raziel introduced secret spiritual exercises, which I give you in this book with a lot of love.
To my infinite joy, that information, which I have shared with you on this site so far and through weekly manifestation messages helped many people change their lives and showed them the way to the conscious creation.It is an infinite joy for me to hear that the messages arrived at the best moment.
This is the order of the Universe, the miracle of the Universe.

How to use the book

At the beginning of the book you will find the Chakra Mapping practice.Print the drawing in the book and use it to mark the areas where you experience blocks.
This figure will show you where you can start.
There are four more exercises on the last pages of the book.
Three practices are designed to remove the energy factors that block manifestation.
Select the one that best suits you and do it.
Apply the practice 2-3 times a week, and review the practice of chakra mapping so that you can see how your energy blocks are cleansed.
The fourth exercise promotes manifestation.
To do it choose an ideal vision of yourself. You can even work with a specific cut. Apply this every day.

When I first met my manifesting guide Archangel Raziel, I had some experiences about manifesting and the law of attraction, but something was missing from my manifestation. I had visions and dreams that hadn't become true, worked on them, but positive results never came.

Was the method that I used wrong, or did I not understand the Law of Attraction? Why did the Law of Attraction not work for me perfectly?
Was the power of manifestation a privilege?
Similar questions came up in my mind. Then half a year later I got the answer to all my question about manifestation, and successfully use the method that I called Angelic Wealth Coaching.

Let's see what Angelic Wealth Coaching means!

Angelic Wealth Coaching

AWC is a multilevel manifestation method which I compiled on the basis of Archangel Raziel's messages to demonstrate the energetic processes of manifestation-

Everything around us is energy. External energies which appear dense in physical form, reflections of our internal energies.
What is inside and out is never contradictory.
When you know the energy patterns in your body, chakras, aura, and recognize the impressions that have created negative beliefs, blocks, and prevented you from living a fulfilling life, you can change them.

During the AWC you will receive information and exercises which will lead you to discovering the blocks to unlocking and supporting manifestation of your new life.
In this manifestation we reactivate the manifestation energy and learn how to use it so that our dreams come true.

This elixir is an angelic energetic method that purifies the energy system, revives and extends the manifestation energy, thus the manifestation of our dreams, and impacts our physical and mental health and DNA.

While working on it, imagine making your wildest dreams come true and getting rid of energetic impressions that prevent your life from unfolding and energy blocks that cause physical illness.

When you apply the method, exercises, and meditations, the DNA pattern will transform as well as your energy pattern. As a result you will live a healthier, richer, happier life.

Angelic Wealth Coaching (as I mentioned earlier) is a multidimensional manifesting method based on knowing the energy system and Angelic Guidance.

Archangel Raziel said that our energy system, the chakras, aura, patterns, memories - our vibration, energy frequencies - determine our future. Our words, thoughts, and feelings create our reality. If we discover these patterns, imprints from past experiences, memories, and let them go, we can develop our manifestation energy, and attract everything we want.

When we feel that something blocks our life emergence and it is impossible to realize our dreams, and no matter how much we want something, nothing happens despite all our efforts, it is worth examining what is in the background, beneath the surface.

Archangel Raziel says:

"What appears outside is never different from what's inside.
It can only appear in physical reality, which is the same as the energy released.
Everything is determined by thought and emotional vibration. There cannot be a thing in your world which you would not have created, what does not match your vibration cannot appear.
You're responsible for your life."

When you delve deeper into the AWC practices, you will notice that symbols will appear in pictures depicting the manifestation and become recognizable in meditations.
You can find the spiral, the infinite sign, and the Caldeus stick which also displays the DNA pattern and kundalini.

How can the Manifestation Process be described on the Chakras Level?

The chakras are energy centers along the spine.
In order to create a conscious manifestation, these energy centers must be in harmony with each other - they need to have the same frequency information.
When the energy centers are dirty with negative imprints and patterns, the process of manifestation becomes difficult.
But when we cleanse the currents from negative blocking patterns from bottom to top and back and accept the possibilities of manifestation, the two streams of the DNA pattern stream through the chakras freely and we create a clean path to manifestation of our dreams.

When this alignment takes place, it affects not only the manifestation of our dreams, but also our physical and spiritual wellbeing and the DNA pattern changes.
Can you imagine what this means?
Can you imagine what great things you'd be capable of if you had the ability to consciously purify and control your energies?

A little background...

My childhood dream was that I become no 1 bestselling author and I know I will create a method, that can help everyone all over the world to manifest their dream and change their life.

My parents supported my dream, but the others said: *you can't do it; you are a very silly girl, what you image, that is not reality. It is impossible.*

I loved the writing. Books, papers, notes, pen, and pencil surrounded me. My room was such a writing sanctuary.

Then I married, we moved a little village in Hungary and we created a farm. Our financial situation wasn't good, we live without electricity 4 years.

My dream, then I become no 1 bestselling author started to fade away.

Have you felt, then you are at a low point from where is it impossible to stand up? Have you ever felt that the world has conspired against you, and you can't do anything?

You are sitting in your room and unable to see the victimhood. Don't like your life, your circumstances and you almost give up...

I started from that state.

I remember, one day I was sitting in my herbs garden and meditating.

I hear a voice: *"Embrace it! Embrace it with love. If you don't like your circumstances, change it! Start to love and embrace them."*
This message was my life-saver.

Three and half years passed and I am here. My life changed.
12 years ago I have read a book and watch the movie, called The Secret. Did you see or read anyone?
This book and movie were a very deep impact for me. My favorite expert of this film: Dr. Joe Vitale.
When I saw the movie, I made a decision: I will learn from Joe Vitale.
I use the Law of Attraction. I made the vision board for years to years, I meditate and visualize my goals, dreams, but the change doesn't happen.
After my experience of my herbs garden change something.

It happens in three and half years ago.

I developed an own method, called Teraxlation, what based on my message, the power of the heart, transbreathing, and gratitude. But it was not enough.

I learn a lot and I used some different method, while in 2015 (In the two thousand fiftheen) I got an opportunity to become the co-author of Patricia LeBlanc.

I think a lot of it. It was my dream, and I worked on it a lot. But I afraid of the language mistake. My mother tongue is Hungarian.

One of my friends persuasion me, and I said yes.

It was my turning point.

Until this point not was big changes in my life. The days spent day by day and I use the different methods but in the background, I struggled with lack of self-confidence, lack of money, and my soul insurances.

My manifestation does not bring awesome success.

Why didn't manifest until this point anything that I want? What was the missing piece?

Raziel Archangel gave the answers.

This program main goal is to deliver some instantly useful and powerful practices and show how can you develop your manifestation skills with the energy-clearing and using visualization and Ho'oponopono.

I will show the two energy flow in your body and give some delightful information about Law of Attraction.

Everybody has different blocks what holding back and blocked the process of manifestation.
I also had and still have now.
In my herbs garden I recognize them, but one of question: How can I leave my negative feelings, emotions what caused by my life experiment or how can I change my beliefs which I live in day by day?
Archangel Raziel shows some way how can we change our life and how can we step out of the darkness hours of the soul.
If we recognize our beliefs and stored negative energy we can able to change the reality of our life.
The law of attraction works. But what I experience it in the last years and during the conversation with Archangel Raziel, but we need to let go of our blocks.

How can we see our blocks, how can we recognize them?
Where are stored, and how they can able to develop and control to our life?

The beliefs, emotions, experience, memories are stored in our body, muscles, mind, heart, and energy system. They stored in our chakras.

If we see the process of manifestation, we can watch our body & muscles, mind, heart and energy system play maintain role. They are the basis.
If you know what would you like to manifest in your life, but something is not matched with your dream, the manifestation will be hard.

Archangel Raziel said:

"The clearing of the energy system is the best practices to develop your manifesting skills.
You are able to create anything that you want. You were born to the creation of your life. This information, this skills, this ability, this blessing is stored inside you. If you forget who you are, where come from, what would you do with love, what is your passion, what is the divine purpose your life, your energy system is blocked. Full of negative things. It obstacles that you see clearly, and do it your divine work from the inspiration.
These blocks of your energy system prevent your contact with the Universe, with God, Goddess, Angels, so they block the blessed rain what develop your true self."

and, where and how begins the manifestation?

Universal Laws and Manifestation

You will fully understand the Angelic Wealth Coaching-Manifesting with Archangel Raziel method, learn about some universal laws, and understand how the energies play a role in your life.

The Law of Unity: we are all one. We are linked by an invisible energetic field and this field affects everything. Everything connects with everything.
The butterfly effect confirms this principle.

The Law of Forgiveness: when you clearly understand what forgiveness means energetically, you'll recognize that this is the most important thing in the Stream of Liberation.
When you forgive someone, you liberate yourself from a negative force. When you forgive yourself, you are ready to begin a new life.

Forgiveness is a clearing method. If you use this power, your life will become better and healthier.

You will see in this method how the energy of forgiveness affects your health and how liberates you from a negative relationship and supports the process of manifestation.

The Law of Gratitude: when you focus on gratitude and seek what you can thank for in your life, the door to miracles will open. You will experience a lot of wonderful things in your life and get more energy.
The energy of gratitude is wonderful and really life changing.
Gratitude has magnetic power which is able to manifest everything you want. Just focus on what you have, be grateful for it, and the universe will give you more magical things.

The Law of Attraction: responses all thoughts, feelings, words. It gives everything you want. Ask and you will be given.

When I asked Archangel Raziel what were the most important universal laws with regard to this method, he said:

"All universal laws are important in your life and the process of manifestation. But you can see the manifestation based on the centre of your heart, love, and responsibility.

If you accept unity, you can take responsibility for your life and the world, because you know that everything is connected. Your thought effects others' lives, just as when a butterfly flaps its wings, it can cause a storm on the other side of the world.
It's based on love and the centre of your heart. When you're angry, the manifesting power of your heart is reduced.
It loses vibration, and low vibrations attract low results. When you forgive someone or something, you release your anger, your heart will be liberated from negative energy, and its vibration will grow."

Have you ever experienced Reiki or other energy healing?
When I learnt Reiki, my teacher showed me an interesting exercise.
One of the students lay on a massage table and our teacher used Reiki.
She put her hand above the student's heart and asked her to think of someone who hurt her. The teacher said "imagine this person, and say: I forgive you. I liberate you. I forgive myself. I liberate myself from all negative energy of our relationship. Thank you for being a part of my life. I love you".

When the student said I love you, the teacher's hand raised up. Because the heart's energy / magnetic field is bigger than the mind, when you forgive, your heart is liberated from negative energy and its vibration grows.

Archangel Raziel said that the law of forgiveness was based on the centre of the heart.
Gratitude is an awesome expression of your love. It has magical and huge power. Gratitude causes miracles in your life.
Gratitude is based on love and the centre of your heart, and it also determines your perspetive.

The Law of Attraction is based on the vibration that you emit to the universe.
The universe gives everything that you want. It responds to your thoughts, words, feelings.
It responds to your energy.
If you vibrate in low frequencies, you'll get things that match your frequency.
If you liberate yourself from negative energy (the Law of Forgiveness), accept responsibility for your life, experience the feeling of unity (you can see in the symbol of Infinity), and focus on gratitude in your life, you can consciously apply the Law of Attraction to manifest wonderful things in your life.

The law of attraction is also based on love and the centre of your heart.
Let see how energy plays an important role in the manifesting process.

A little energetic background...

The field is an electromagnetic space which is universal and everywhere.
The manifesto is done in this field or in the universe.
In this space the manifestation energy is thickened into energy as a physical form, and this is where everything happens.
If you look at the picture, how is creation created? Through this method you can see the chakras, the aura, and the universal space outside our bodies which surrounds them.
We are now deeper into the chakras and the aura as we are starting out from the energy base of creation.
When dealing with the chakras and aura, you get to know the universal field and what causes changes in it more deeply.
It's like the butterfly effect.
You change an idea, a mind vibration, the frequency of a word, the cause of an act, and will see corresponding changes in the world.

The Chakras

Have you ever wondered that, if all the energy around us and the energies of our thoughts, feelings, and words create our reality and are the energy system of our body, our chakra, our energy field what role does it play in conscious creation?

If communication and creation begin at an energetic level, how do our energy centers with negative impressions influence manifestation, the formation of our life?

Can you imagine the secret of your energy system?
What kind of imprints do you have?
What do you think, can for example, the problem of sacral chakra (eg infertility) be related to the third step of the Law of Attraction?

How does our energy system support conscious creation?
How do cleaning our chakras and liberating energy currents affect the manifestation and how do they heal illnesses, relationships, and financial problems?

The chakras form a continuous chain in the line of our spine.
They interact with each other, affect each other, and every inner soul voice.
The operation and harmony of the chakras, or when balance among them is lost influences all that which is manifested in the outer world.

What's inside is outside.
These energy centers are responsible for our physical and mental health.
Chakras, as energy centers, generate and store energy and information. Everything that happens to us, our thoughts, others' thoughts, our and others' experiences appear as impressions in our chakras and the electromagnetic field around us. When I asked Archangel Raziel about stored patterns, he said that all patterns that have ever affected us indirectly or directly in our energy centers and all that can be found in our energy field (chakra and aura) has an impact on life.

When we change a thought, the energy and quality of the chakras change.
When we switch from one emotion to another, our vibrations change, thus of course there is a change in the chakras, which translates into the outer world as visible energetic changes.

When chakras run below their capacity due to being contaminated with negative imprints, it has a debilitating effect on the body, creates imbalance in health, and weakens the conscious use of manifesting energy.

The energy field is the energetic subconscious of our body.
Are our beliefs and patterns leaving energetic impressions on our bodies?
Can our obsolete beliefs and patterns be perceived on the energetic level?

The patterns dissolved in the energy system, and the practice of dissolving negative imprints can liberate us from suffering and obstacles caused by negative belief system.It can also bring deeper spiritual understanding and self-knowledge.

Imagine an intelligent flow between energy centers.
Continuous flow of communication does not just happen between two chakras, but among all the cells of our body.
Thanks to this continuously flowing energy we are fit, happy, healthy, HEARTY, and this harmoniously functioning energy flow helps our growth and creation of wellbeing through conscious use of manifestation energy.

Let's see what happens when a chakra becomes dirty!
An element which changes the intensity and frequency of the current is added to the system.
For example, there is a situation whereby we lose our inner balance.
This element, this small dust stream travels from one center to the other along the current, thus communication between the chakras changes. If we do not consciously awaken to this change and do not switch to another frequency, the "dust" will stay permanently in the energy system and may grow or deeply embed itself, preventing conscious creation.
Let's see what is the result of deeper embedding of the negative imprint.

Negative situations bring "dust" into the chakra communication system, energy is slower, and its quality is different. Each of the emerging negative situations gets deeper and deeper until the continuity of the current is broken and energy communication flows through a smaller gap.
Observe the electric current. When the wire is flawless, the electricity flows continuously. But if the cable is broken somewhere, the electricity is disconnected.

This fault in the flow of energy impairs conscious manifestation.

Corruption of the communication stream exudes energy of lower frequency into the universe, and according to the Law of Attraction the universe responds to this communication.
This is why negative destructive situations come up again and again in our lives.

During my conversation with Archangel Raziel we created a Chakra Mapping method.
This method is complex.

With a simple meditation we can find the blocks in our energy system, the places where dust had crept into the system.

When we find and discover the deeper causes of our lives, awaken to the blocks, we will be able to liberate ourselves from them.
As we learn to search for our blocks like an Angelic Abundance Coach, we will look for blocks in others and help them resolve them.

When we have done the Chakra-mapping practice, we'll discover hampered communication between many energy centers in the energy system.

Information stored in energy centers affects other information by cause and effect. You can lift the other chakras, thus the quality of the radiated energy, but it can be extremely weakened by it.

When the frequency is high and nourishing, we feel able to influence our lives and do anything we can to create whatever we want. When we change to a lower frequency, it can easily attract the victim's role, as this frequency can only create similar situations through the radiated energy quality.

But knowing all this I have great news.

We can change the situation.

We can unlock the blocks and reactivate continuous nutritious communication in our energy system. This reactivation will be a release not only on the energetic level, but it will also be free from negative impressions, and we will be alsoable to cure physical symptoms of diseases.

We will become able to consciously change DNA patterns.

Can you imagine what this means?

Exercise 1
Chakra Mapping meditation

Please use this meditation, and mark on the chakra card where you felt that the energy was impeded.
Close your eyes, take a deep breath, relax your body.
Let go of everyday problems and tasks from your mind.
Breathe deeply through your crown chakra, lead along the spine, breathe through the root chakra.
Inhale through the crown chakra, Ride along the vertebral column, exhale through the root chakra.
Once more inhale through the crown chakra, ride along the spine, and slowly breathe out through the root chakra.
Imagine how a silver light from Mother Earth's womb begins to spiral upward in your body.
The spiral of silver energy goes from chakra to chakra.
Watch the flow.
The flow is intense, slow, uniform or blocked, barrier-free.
Listen to your feelings and let this magical energy go up all over your energy center.

Imagine how it passes through the root chakra, sacral chakra, reaches the solar chakra, passes through the heart chakra, throat chakra, the third eye, and reaches the crown chakra and connects with the universe and the Source.
Take a deep breath, move your fingers, and open your eyes.

Let's look at what this energy map tells you

The energies of our thoughts, emotions, words, and actions affect our lives. They affect the quality of our manifestation and its the result.
The Law of Attraction responds to the vibration emitted by us, while the radiated vibration is determined by information stored in us, our chakras, our minds, our hearts, and memories.

When I first talked to Archangel Raziel about manifestation and how energy affected our creation, he told me the following things.
Energy is an integral part of manifestation.
Our thoughts, words, feelings, the quality of vibration, the extent of the energy field around us, the status of our chakra influence this creation.
When something we want to accomplish in our life is very important, that is the desire, the idea to be perfectly consistent with us.
It is not enough to visualize the wonderful things flowing to us. We also have to cut them to a wavelength.

If you'd like to have a million in your bank account but you do not have a bank account and do not want to open one, then are you on the same wavelength with your goal?

No.
If you want magical moments with your lover but have a phobia of men and do not appreciate and you respect yourself as a woman, are you on the same wavelength with your desire?

No.

You feel a craving and resistance.

This resistance can be conscious or subconscious.
It can be based on a belief, you can find it in an experience, memory, your energy system.
It can be recognizable and dissolvable.

When you hold a counter-energized energy imprint on your chakra, aura, it reduces the quality and power of your manifestation energy.

I'll tell you a story. My son was born 20 years ago.
He was 4 years old when we moved to the farm.
My husband went to work, I raised the baby.
I bred animals, I did homework. In the first two years water was in the spit cavity.

To feed the animals, cook, or wash myself in the apartment I had to draw water from a well several times a day, and carry buckets into the apartment.

All my dreams were to have one more child. I was pregnant, but miscarried.

One year later I got pregnant again, but miscarried again.

Doctors said that it was due to incompatibility of genes.

In that year we started renovating the farm and I enrolled in a drawing-psychology course.

One task on the course was to draw a figure, a person. Then a figure of the other gender.

I did the job and turned in my drawings.

The child question was very pressing, so we went to one doctors after another, but got no sensible answer to the problem from anyone.

We were nearing the end of the drawing psychology course when the instructor took our pictures out and we started analyzing them.

We had people on our drawings. The instructor put up my first drawing.

My team members started analyzing.

"He's strong, yes, he's physically strong, he's a definite man, he does a menial job."

I was shocked by the real cause of my infertility:

I had taken the male role on the farm upon myself. I worked like a man. A man does not give birth to a baby...

For years there was this imprint in my energy field. For the sake of consciousness this poisonous thought generated a few other unpleasant low-vibrational thoughts, and literally blocked the path of my physical manifestation of desire.

I wanted to have a baby, but all my thoughts and actions were of a man. I was not on the wavelength of that dream. The frequencies were opposing.
When Archangel Raziel spoke of the role of the chakras in manifestation, he said that the sacral chakra played a major role in the reception of things.
He explained that this was the energy field which provided fertile or infertile soil for the desert dream core. From there the development of the seed would start or be thrown away.

If you wish to achieve the well-being necessary to keep your energy clean, you need to keep balance in your chakras.
The radiated energy determines the quality of the results.

How can you enjoy pleasant experiences and create angelic abundance in your life if your energy field is dirty with negativity?

The creative force is blessed with the same energy works, like a radio transmitter: It transmits the frequency at which you set it.

Would you like to implement abundance, interact with the angels, and experience manifestation as described in the previous section?
A quality power is required from within.
The aura embracing your body and the chakras store pieces of your events, thoughts, feelings, energies.

Like attracts like.

What you emit from yourself, the universe reflects back to you.
If your thoughts, words, actions reflect deficit, loss of sensation, victimhood, low vibration frequency, the energy that you emit will transmit this so that the universe cannot guarantee you anything more than these feelings, thoughts, and energy.
This energy will not attract abundance. It will allow diseases to enter an extraordinary way of life.

The angels say that *"the ability to create abundance is highly dependent on the energy vibration of the quality of our words; the beliefs that we develop about money, material possessions, and wealth.*
The energy is a storage system of information, of which the stock includes everything imprinted, like the subconscious.
That is, in and out, the flow never conflicts.
In this life the material life happens in the event of the background story which can be found in our subconscious and energy system.
When you begin to trace the dominant thoughts, when you create your own description of abundance and form belief-about it, you take a huge step forward on the path of abundance."

However, this is not all.

Not only your words and thoughts, but also all your chakras need cleaning from the dirt that has clung to them over the years.
I think that one of the greatest blessings in our lives is the ability to consciously change, which, although it requires perseverance and consistency, will produce a result that will never lag behind.

How can we purify our thoughts, feelings, beliefs from negativity? How can overwrite our fears? How can we increase the quality of our energies in order to connect with the flow of abundance?

"The universe provides everything for you. Everything necessary to live happy and fulfilling lives.
It will give you all the sounds and gestures that direct attention to prosperity.
The Universe invites you to dance with abundance which ensures the flow and the corresponding occurrence of miracles in your life.
The key is still in you.
It is the key which allows you the conscious recognition of this amazing fact.
The vision begins in the heart. What you are hiding in your heart, the balance of love or fear, is reflected in everything you see.
If you like the universe and honour the all-encompassing abundance, notice the signs - you'll be able to flow along in wellbeing. If, however, your actions, thoughts, words are based on fear, you will be unable to swim freely with the flow.
For as long as you trade your feelings based on fear / deficits you will experience this as power quality results.

The key is in your hands at all times.
Do you choose love or fear?
Overflowing abundance which comes to others, or closed fingers over a fistful of cash?
Joyful wellbeing or lack of closure in jail?
Cleanse yourself!
Discover the paralyzing chains, look for their names, and let them go!
Sort through the mental and emotional energy that they emit. Add positive content to your words directed towards the Bountiful.
Improve your posture, validate your muscles near the spine, because when your posture improves the body's stance, it also strengthens the roots.
Generous welfare loves a secure basis. "

Proper functioning of our chakras is very important for the use of manifestation (materialization) of energy.

Each energy center actively contributes to the process of manifestation, to shaping our future.
In this section you will find a brief description illustrating how and what role our chakras play in conscious creation.

Everything is connected. Everything draws energy from the other. It gives energy and energy is lost in a constant cycle.

The chakras, these rotating power centers, communicate in the language of energy along the spine.
The radiated energy is used to form waves of information from them.
The communication of the chakras is a fundamental element of the manifest.

Imagine an idea that formed in your mind.
Imagine that this idea is the core of a constantly pulsating vibrant ball of energy.
Things all around us are made up of energy.
The movement also applies to the power of the Law of Attraction:
Like attracts like.
A ball of energy that carries the chair pattern includes never having been connected with any power, ensuring the physical appearance of the door.
The outer shell of the energies that surround the core varies. Its size and quality change depending on the effects.

Let's look at the energy of abundance:

There is a ball of energy and it has an essential core that awakened from the abundance.
This core starts to grow, forms a fertile field around itself, and the seeds in it grow.

This core, however, can be found in nature's plant seeds in germination.
If the productive power receives other round effects, the primary energy - the essential core - will be available at any time.
External influences over us in the background are also energy.
A cause of all the consequences is an energy blast.
Positive or negative energy blast.

The law of cause and effect affects everything - explosions and discharges of energy.

Just see for yourself when waves of vibrating energies of peace suddenly connect to an energy news which causes you anger.
You have a choice: return to the peace powers or let your angry energies envelope the main core of energy.

When you clean and channel your energies, you will feel the flow of life and experience incredible coincidences which will lead to progress in your life.
The process of achieving this is the primary energy of your desire, goal, dream.

The sacral chakra is the fertile soil for helping to increase the energy of your dream.

The root chakra provides the roots, the sacral chakra receives your dreams. The sacral chakra enables being able to live through the realization of the dream inspired steps.

Can you accommodate this in front of the unfolding stream of wellbeing? Or do you block the life nurturing energies that influence the energy field around your body?
It is the key to the science of creation.

The Two Flow

It is astonishing that millions of people are trying to apply the Law of Attraction to realization of their dreams and fight for living rich and abundant lives, while others simply, playfully, and cheerfully attract everything they want.
Do you know what this is all about?
For years I have been looking for answers to how we can apply conscious creation in our daily lives.
How can we control our creative power without struggles, which is our birth right, not a privilege.
I sought the answer to how we can achieve financial freedom.
The simplest things are the greatest.
But the simplest things seem to be complicated for many people.

Ask.
Believe.
Receive.
But first of all, clear your beliefs which block the implementation.

When we look at manifestation from the perspective of the energy system and the energetic processes in the body, we can see the two interconnecting streams.

The *flow of liberation:*
from root chakra to crown chakra
and
the *Manifesting flow*:
from crown to root chakra.

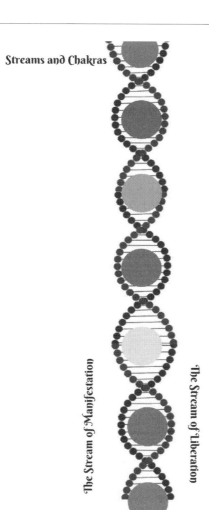

The upward stream helps to recognize our beliefs / dominant thoughts, and good practices support the release, the blocking of nodules.

The flow of manifestation through inspiration from the Universe, from crown to root chakra to a dense form of material, it helps the manifesto by interconnecting the two spirally flowing streams that we imagined.

Each energy center includes a special area, all the events that have ever occurred in our life, our energy imprint (deeper layers store the previous life info), which subconsciously influence the quality of our existence. The words and thoughts of others have an impact on us, a continuous recurring pattern in our energy system, which leads to recurring events and cycles.

When we feel that we cannot do something, the dream is not realized, and the Law of Attraction seems to be against us, we must exit the cycle and change the pattern.

The Law of Attraction is neutral. It responds to the vibrations we emit. It has nothing to do with us, or against us, it simply manifests in the physical world all that, which is inside.

When you clean your chakras and your energy field from all the energies that are not good for you and block your process of creation, you get closer to your dreams.

When they are intensified, they are balanced, cleansed by your chakras, emitted
(perceptible in the aura), and specific energy will gain strength.

When you charge this energy consciously to your dreams, you will accelerate with high frequency.
You will support the process of manifestation.
Ask for cleansing in the area.
The light of your cleansed chakras directs the desired thing.
(Connect it energetically) fill your desire with the amazing stream of high energies.
The light of the rainbow cures, awakens, defends, and with special attractiveness gives it to you.
When this connection through the chakras occurs, the law of energy awakens your desires.
This swirl gets bigger and bigger thanks to energy.
Feed this vortex with the mantra:
„My dreams come true"

Charged energy attracts all the situations and people who help things to come true.

Cleaning the energy system not only increases physical wellbeing, but also supports active and constructive use of your Manifestation Energy.

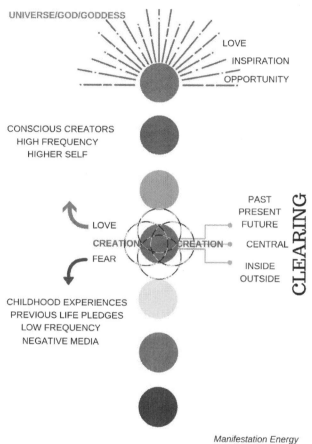

Manifestation Energy

Chakras and Manifestation

The root chakra includes our beliefs, family patterns, social expectations.
These beliefs positively or negatively affect the process of manifestation.
These fixed ideas (which are clearly reflected in our minds) can be said to serve as a craving for our desirable things.
When the seed, our desires, dreams, and the seeds of our desires fall into fertile soil, the sacred chakra is incapable of dreaming, and we can get the same nutrition as the solar plexus from the bottom of the root chakra (our beliefs).
The root chakra gives "terrestrial" energies, and the solar chakra conveys the "energies of heaven".
When the sacral chakra is blocked and does not work properly, not only does the dream-carrying ability decrease, but even fertility problems may appear.

The solar chakra is responsible for transmitting "heavenly" energy. Blessed with rain, it educates the dreaming hearts admitted by the sacral chakra, supporting the inner day.

In case of a blockage the will for ego, selfish energies, and the desire of power and control - in many cases ready for dispatch - leads to dehydration of the dream core.
If this area conveys the "blessed rain", the ego will be a guide in the background and the cramped desire will transform into the birth of a greater force.

When working on the bottom three chakras, to become a co-creator of the universe / God / angels in conscious creation the faith to ask and give is strengthened. The heart chakra is the center of creation and the energy system. This center has an electromagnetic space 50 times stronger than the brain.

When the lower (root, sacral, solar) and the upper (crown, forehead (third eye, throat) chakras are in balance, the energy of the heart chakra (the creative energy) becomes powerful and the manifestation is transformed into a continuous process.

Balance requires release and acceptance. So the heart chakra is the center of manifestation.

Everyone has the ability to create, but, as we can see, not everyone consciously employs it.

The throat chakra is responsible for expressing ourselves verbally (communication channels).
The thoughts expressed by our communication channel represent a vision.

The vision is consciously from top to bottom.
This means that our thoughts and words are not the basis of vision, but the vision determines what ideas and words we emit into the Universe.
This is a very important moment during manifestation.

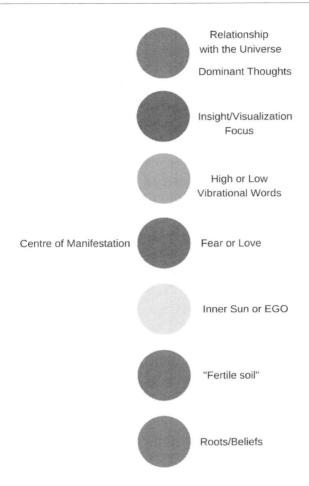

The Root chakra

The *root chakra* plays a very important role in manifestation.
Not only because from this point of view the basis for the purpose to be realized are the beliefs and root ideas, but also because in the last step this helps to realize our vision and final molding.
When the root chakra stores false beliefs about dreams and targets, it cannot nourish manifestation with positive thoughts.
The root chakra is a foundation based on beliefs and dominant thoughts / emotions related to all the subjects inherent in it. This base gives the "basic vibration" of our lives.

Have you ever been in a position when you did everything you could to achieve something, but despite all your efforts it did not materialize? You hit some obstacle...
The three steps of the law of attraction build from bottom to top from this point and from top to bottom in the flow of manifestation.
This means that until you let go of the (perhaps even several generations) deep or "lifelong" beliefs, your dreams will remain blocked.

Ask.
Believe.

Accept.
But first of all do some energetic work, which provides a strong positive foundation for molding.

To have the Law of Attraction applied in your life to the greatest benefit and goodwill and to make your goals come true, crawl it up the area of the root chakra:

- What are your dominant thoughts / feelings about your dream being realized?
- If you recall your childhood / juvenile self, your relationships, family, what you have heard, what emotions do you experience? How do your experiences affect your relationship with that particular area?
- If you look at your beliefs, can you find a stable base on which you can build the life that you dream of?
- Can you provide a quality nutrition stream through the roots of the dream-core you rejected? Can you always supply or nurture energies through the roots chakra to help you develop?

- Do you feel stable and balanced, as if you had roots grow by themselves and provide continuous support and development?
- Is it safe for you to accept what you want? If your dream comes true, could you feel fear and awakened?
- If so, what fears can you bring to life that would reduce your joy and wellbeing?
- Do you take responsibility for things that have been manifested in your life and events?
- Do you believe that you are the creator of your life, or a victim controlled by the outer world? Are you giving your life shape or are others influencing it?

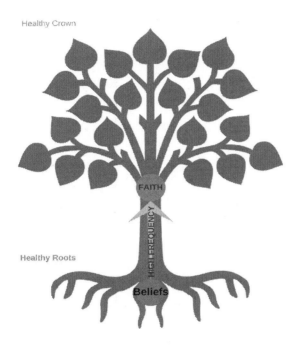

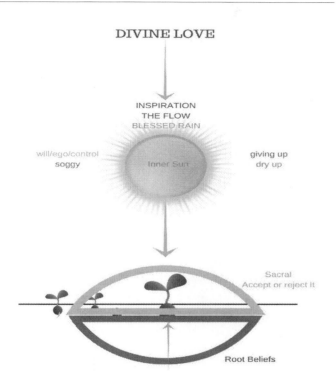

The Sacral Chakra

The sacral chakra is a fertile ground for manifestation.
The dream seeds here are rejected and come to life with proper nutrition.

Feeding flows in two ways:

- through the roots / belief system
- Energies coming through the inner Sun

The solar chakra gives identity, personality, care, contributes to them in the womb, and results in manifesting through the birth canal.
Through this area we can learn more about ourselves, the reactions of the world, and our events.

Here we experience the "blessed state of receiving seed and bringing it to life.
When the sacral chakra works properly, we are able to concentrate on a purpose, we do not slip nor delay; we feel aligned with our business, we cultivate maternal love, protect the miracle that develops in our uterus, knowing that each sewn seed has timing.

We do not want to change the time, we do not induce any external climate change in order to bring our "child" to the world as soon as possible. We know the universe's overall harmony, accepting opportunities which do not speed up, but also the "manifestation ability" of various forms.

- Do you know yourself? Are you aware of deeper layers, strengths, and weaknesses of your personality?
- Do you include new opportunities and methods, or do you have an established belief system on which you insist?
- Are you afraid of change? Can you flow with thoughts that change, can you integrate them into your life.
- Are you attuned or do you care?
- How do you feed your dreams on the path of becoming reality? How much energy do you experience in your daily lives? What energies do you see?
- What energies do you have on cloudy days?
- Do you have essentially masculine or feminine energies or personality traits? How can you bring the two into harmony with each other?

- What does "bringing to the world" mean to you?

The Mystery of Birth is hidden in this chakra. Everything that is manifested in the world is born through this area, and the experience of this process becomes holy or profound.

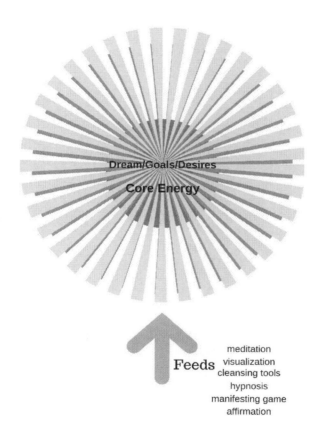

I WOULD LIKE TO MANIFEST...

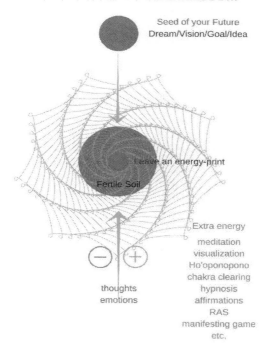

The Solar Chakra

The solar chakra carries the Inner Sun.
The strength that promotes growth.
The power that many people identify as power and control, while energetically and spiritually the term means just the opposite - coupled with the chakra below and above it.

When the solar chakra works properly, we are able to give more of ourselves in the process of implementation, and coupled with the heart chakra, we awaken and bow to the truth of the universal laws. We examine, accept, and connect with our existence.

Our desire is fuelled by the ego (fear, control of life, dominating situations, control) or the wonderful energy of the inner day.In the process of manifestation egoistic thoughts are used as nourishing powers in this energy center.

You will notice that we are tired of the struggle for implementation and are moving forward; we are unable to flow with the universe and live in constant convulsion, and always focus on performance, but the results achieved are not properly evaluated.

We desire to satisfy one desires one after another, and need (shortage) motivates us instead of love.

When we feed the Inner Sun, we align with the Source of our lives in blessed leadership to get events to accelerate and our worlds become wonders. We see synchronicities and feel peace. The idea of dispatch, the ego's idea also comes from the solar chakra. Giving up means that you are away from your dream and will not take any further steps to achieve it. If you do not trust in yourself and it, the universe will support anything.

(This feeling will be the core of the victim's role).

In contrast, surrender to accepting the ever-flowing energy of the Infinite Source, and you'll be close to love.

- What are your feelings when you meet a person who has reached the goal you want to achieve?
- What are your dominant thoughts about manifestation?
- What are your first thoughts when they say: "Does the universe support you in realizing your dream at all times?"

- What do you think when you hear that there are no coincidences? And why did you attract this and that to happen in your life?
- Where do you come from? Love or fear (thoughts of shortage)? What is your basis for your goals?
- Control or drive, dominance, or flow, which is closer to you?
- When someone gives you advice, how do you feel about it? Can you listen to it, integrate it into your life, coordinate it with your personality, or feel internal protests, which you may be able to declare?

Your Inner Sun is a life-giving light that manifests or dries others' thoughts.

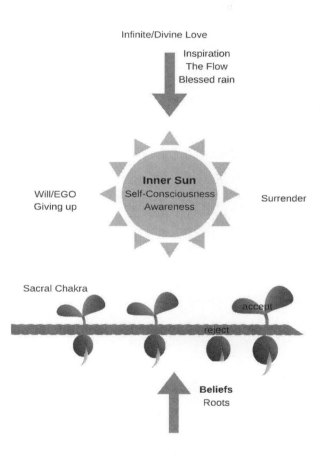

The Heart Chakra

In our hearts the Earth meets Heaven, this area is the central actor in the present moment and manifestation energy.
In this chakra we keep the faith in God, the universe, angels. hence the miracles of the most majestic human feelings.

The manifested energy evolving here transmits our vibrations as signals to the universe to start dreaming about starting the attitude process.
This area is energetically considered the most intense, the magnetic field is 5000 times larger than the mind.

Many misunderstood the teachings of the Law of Attraction.
They thought that it was enough to break the thoughts in the mind, while their feelings, faith, beliefs were in the opposite direction.
In order for energy to manifest, which is a divine part of your life, you must fully use the expressed requests, faith, beliefs, and thoughts and emotions must be aligned.

When you experience balance, the gates will be opened and what you want will become realistic.

The heart has the opportunity to experience the present moment, which is the perfect time for manifestation.

- What is your relationship with the world around you?
- How do you think about your circumstances? When you look at your manifested world, what are your feelings?
- Do you accept, love, and are grateful for all that has come to your life so far, or do you object to it?
- How do you proclaim your appreciation of your manifested world and gratitude?
- What is your connection with the universe?
- How do you think of the Source, God, angels?
- Are you able to follow an open mind and heart with an invisible life-changing force?
- Do you love, respect, accept, and appreciate yourself? How would you describe your relationship with yourself?

In the energetic process of manifestation the Holy Mother is Godmother and Mother Goddess in the heart, and in this sacred love the energy of creation is saturated with energy.

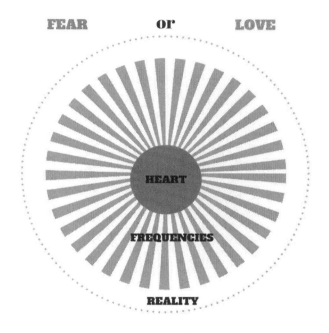

"The magnetic field of the HEART center is 5,000-times stronger than the magnetic field of the brain."

HeartMath Institute

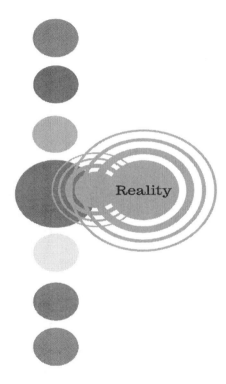

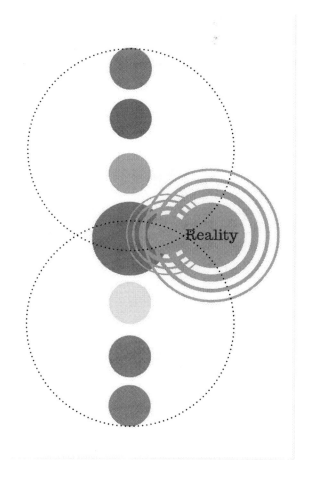

The Troat Chakra

The throat chakra as the center of communication where words used to express thoughts (verbal and nonverbal communication) are a bridge to what we want to manifest.
Every spoken and unspoken thought emits rays of energy into the universe.
These rays have high or low vibrations .
This means that your thoughts with high vibration are full of love, gratitude, and evaluation, are associated with appropriate things, events, people, and these feelings are constantly evolving in your life.
When deficit fills the dominant role in your words of complaint, the universe responds to your energy radiations with corresponding things.

- Which words do you use most often in communication with yourself?
- How do you characterize yourself in such communication?
- How do you communicate with others?
- What kind of communication do you prefer
- How would you describe the bridges that you built within yourself and with others?

- What do you think about the communication bug? Has there been a situation in your life when you stepped off the floor of communication?
- Do you pay attention to improving the flow of information around you?
- What words do you use with the thing you want to manifest?

Thoughts become words....

High vibrational words = Awesome results

Low vibrational words = Bad results

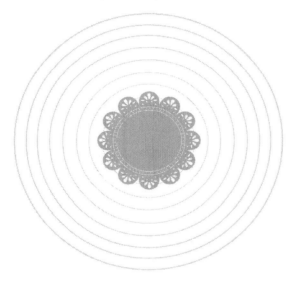

Low vibrational words come from the Fear

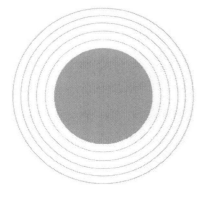

High vibrational words come from the Love

The Third Eye Chakra

The role of the forehead (third eye) chakra in manifestation is to create inner and outer sight.
When we visualize our dreams as if they had already been realized, we develop neurones responsible for imaging and a center of vision in the brain.
This can be seen in two ways:
- After meditation / visualization we see the colours more saturated, as if everything had become brighter.
- Mentally generated images create new nerve paths in the mind.

The visualized experiences and memories are imprinted, by which these images are placed in the focus of vision.

- What you see with your inner eyes you see in reality too.
- What is your focus on your current situation?
- When you look around, what's your visual experience like?
- If you look at an object or event from outside, what do you see in it? What are you feeling about the sight you experience?

- How fast can you focus on a particular (unpleasant) situation?
- How long are you in it until do you get bored?
- Can you look for a light spot in the most troublesome situation?
- Is your vision based on fear or love? Exterior images are reflections of an inner picture. You can change it.
- What are the current external images you want to change?

DREAMS/VISIONS

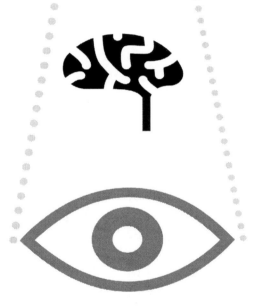

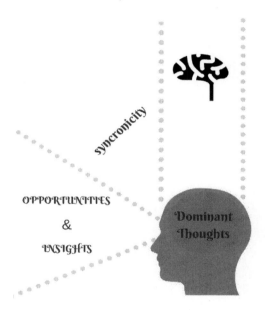

The Crown Chakra

Manifestation takes place in an upward spiral of liberation flow circling the chakras linked with the spiral of the downward manifold flow when there is nothing blocking in the progression of energy.

The crown is the area of higher / deeper spiritual communication (intuition / inspiration).A blocked crown will not open before the messages of the universe, does not recognize them, does not accept them, does not allow them to flow through the energy system.

When this area is cleansed and harmonized with other chakras in the course of liberation, we get closer to the Source. We become the inspired thoughts that support manifestation by pouring the stream into a physical form.

- How do you communicate with the universe / God / angels / the living spirituality that you live with?
- How important is this deeper level of contact to you?
- How does faith relate to the source?
- Are your beliefs / roots allowing this interconnection?

- What are your thoughts on creation and the Divine Creator's power?
- Are you aware of your creative power, mind, and thoughts?
- How do you show this awareness in your life?
- Does your goal drive you from your memories or inspiration?

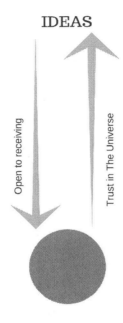

How to Clear your Chakras from the Blocks

We have just seen what role our chakras play in manifestation. Let's look at the negative energy impressions and the beliefs they contain. How do they prevent our dreams from being realized?

How do these energy impressions came about, how can they be recognized, and how can we overwrite them?

How can we clean not only our energy system, but also our minds from them?

We introduce two methods that identify the blocks.

One is a simple basic manifestation practice that, in addition to showing you which chakra does not work properly during manifestation, helps to coordinate the work of the two active streams needed for manifestation.

As we have seen the two streams are:

the flow of liberation / release that flows through the root chakra and crown chakra and helps get rid of negative beliefs

the flow of manifestation that ranges from the crown to the root chakra and helps sleep more deeply to be physically manifested.

When you start flowing in the flow of liberation, spiral energy (toward your request to the universe) near the chakras is where the energy seems to be.
If there is a block, protrusion, or obstacle, it is more difficult to flow through energy.
Where you see the blocks, you find obstacles to the success of your manifestation.

Exercise 2.
Cleaning the aura with Archangel Raziel

Sit down on a chair and get comfortable.
Close your eyes. Ask Archangel Raziel to be here with you and use the colors of the rainbow to clean your aura from all contamination, negative memories, thoughts that prevent your development of manifestation energy and block your dreams from coming true.
Imagine that rainbow ribbons circulate in your body and release the astral flaws under the burden.
While Archangel Raziel cleans your aura using the rainbow ribbons, you begin to repeat the purification terms of Ho'oponopono:
I love you;
I am sorry ;

Please forgive me;
Thank you.
Imagine that these expressions spiral around your body and fill your aura with high vibration energies.
Stay in this charging state for as long as it's good, then thank Archangel Raziel.
Take a deep breath and open your eyes.

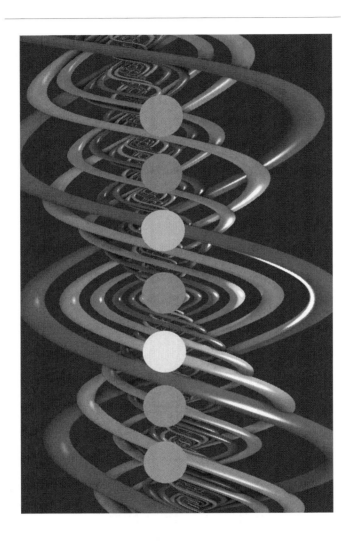

Exercise 3
Grounding and clearing

Make yourself comfortable
It is best to choose a sitting position.
Close your eyes, take a deep breath, and imagine that roots grow from the roots chakra to Mother Earth.
These roots connect with earthly energies and connect with the nourishing ancient power.
The gentle energies of Mother Earth flow to Father Sun through your energy center.
Imagine that branches of deer antlers will reach Father Sun.
The branches, like arms, are received in the sky with love and transmit the energy to Mother Earth through their energy center.
The nourishing energy of Mother Earth meets the energy of Father Sun in the heart chakra, and in this meeting the perfect equilibrium state is born.

Now imagine that Mother Earth's energy stream is a silver spiral up the vertex. The spiral leads from the root chakra through the sacred, solar, heart, and throat chakras to the third eye and crown until the silver spiral reaches the Infinite Force.
Father Sun responds to Mother Earth's message with a golden spiraling energy flow.

The golden energy spirals through the crown chakra, the third eye, the throat, heart, solar, sacred, and root chakras to Mother Earth.

The rising current indicates in which area the energy flow is blocked during manifestation, drawing attention to the fact that it is necessary to start a cleansing treatment in the affected areas.

When you want something and work for it continuously, but the result is dragging, you probably have an imprint in your energy system, an astral trace that hinders fulfillment. You can find it in this practice.

So the upstream flow helps to appeal to the Universe / God / Angels without fear.

The downstream current, the flow of manifestation.

As the energy flows down from the potential of the Father / Universe / God and becomes more and more dense, it gets closer to physical manifestation.

When you detect a block in this stream, i.e. manifestation is caused by blockage of reception, blocks can be felt in both streams in most cases.

When you have cleansed and aligned the two streams, you become more open to receiving inspired messages. With an open heart you have an open mind and faith, welcome with gratitude, and take an inspired step when inspirational steps lead to opportunities.
Now we know how the aura can be cleaned by Archangel Raziel and Ho'oponopono.
We also know how to map blocking in the energy system.
Now let's look at how to clean the energy system from the information stored in it and how manifestation becomes a great and easy process.
Stay sitting.
Close your eyes and imagine the upward flowing silver energy.
While energy flows from chakra to chakra, repeat the following:
I love you.
I'm sorry.
Please forgive me.
Thank you.
Clean all chakras in the release stream with the terms.

Exercise 4
Chakra clearing with the spiral

Get comfortable and close your eyes. Take a deep breath through your crown chakra, hold it, and let it out though your root chakra.
You are love.
Take another deep breath through your crown chakra, hold it, and exhale slowly through your root chakra.
You are the light.
Take a deep breath through the crown chakra, hold it, and let it out through your root chakra.
You are love.
See your root chakra and see a red spiral starting to flow in this energy center. The flowing spiral cleans this area, liberates you from all negative beliefs, and your chakra is shining in an awesome red colour. Put your hand on the area of the root chakra and say:

I love you.
I am sorry.
Please forgive me.
Thank you.
I am love.
I am the light.

Focus on your sacral chakra. See an orange spiral flowing in this chakra and cleaning and liberating you from all negative energy. Your sacral chakra is shining in a wonderful orange colour.
Put your hand on this area and say:

I love you.
I am sorry.
Please forgive me.
Thank you.
I am love.
I am the light.

See your solar chakra. A yellow spiral starts to flow into this area and liberates it from negative imprints and egoistic thoughts, Your solar chakra is shining in awesome yellow, like the sun.
Put your hand on this centre and say:

I love you.
I am sorry.
Please forgive me.
Thank you.
I am love.
I am the light.

Focus on your heart chakra. A shining green spiral starts to flow into this chakra, and clear and liberate it from negative emotions and feelings. The spiral completely cleans it. Your heart chakra enchants in a magical green colour.
Put your hand on the area of the heart chakra and say:

I love you.
I am sorry.
Please forgive me.
Thank you.
I am love.
I am the light.

Put your attention on your throat chakra. See a wonderful light blue spiral starting to flow into it and clean it from all negative words, things, imprints.
Put your hand on this area and say:

I love you.
I am sorry.
Please forgive me.
Thank you.
I am love.
I am the light.

See your third eye chakra. Feel a magical indigo light starting to flow into this area. This swirling light cleans your chakra, your visions, and liberates you from all negative feelings, emotions, thoughts.
Put your hand on the area of the third eye chakra and say:

I love you.
I am sorry.
Please forgive me.
Thank you.
I am love.
I am the light.

Focus on your crown chakra. Imagine a purple spiral starting to flow into this chakra and clean and liberate it from all negative thoughts, and create an awesome relationship with the universe/God/angels.
Put your hand on the area of your crown and say:

I love you.
I am sorry.
Please forgive me.
Thank you.
I am love.
I am the light.
Relax and enjoy this moment.

Take a three deep breaths, move your fingers, and open your eyes. Your energy system is clear and your chakras are balanced.

Exercise 5
Become Conscious Creator

Imagine walking on a forest trail. You are surrounded by trees, bushes, chirping birds.
Fragrant flowers are opening along the path.
You go straight ahead. You're breathing continuously.
You are more and more relaxed.
You're coming to a field.
In the middle of the field you see a stone spiral.
This is the spiral of existence.
The spiral of true being, real life, the sanctuary of your true self.
The direction of the spiral is clockwise.
Go to the spiral.
Go along the stones slowly.
Let go of your feelings, liberate your heart.
Let go of your thoughts, liberate your mind.
As you progress towards the center of the spiral, you are getting more and more relaxed. You're getting cleaner.

You're getting rid of thoughts and feelings and physical barriers.
You're letting go of everything.
When you arrive at the center, you are your real self.
There are no limiting emotions, thoughts, only light and love.
Only you, the true self released from the thoughts.
Nothing.Everything.
Love and light.
Harmony.
Silence.
Have a good time in this magical moment.
Now imagine the life you want to live in pictures.
Imagine that it is already happening.
See, hear, feel...
Colour the images, dream your life.
Imagine that everything you desire is radiated from your heart chakra in this new life. It is transformed into a wonderful brilliant sphere which smokes.
You are the center of this wonderful brilliant sphere.
Feel your future.
Feel your life.
Enjoy the moment as you become a conscious creator.

Put your hands on your heart and say to yourself: I love you. Thank you. Thank you . Thank you.
Keep this sphere around you, then get back from the spiral center.
As you progress, keep the flame in your heart, in the glittering circle of yourself, love, gratitude, and spell.
Repeat:
I love you.
I am sorry.
Please forgive me.
Thank you.
When you get out of the spiral, you are a new person. Your aura is filled with the seeds and possibilities of a blessed life.
Go back down the forest path.
Slowly go straight on.
Take a deep breath through the crown chakra, hold it, and say:
I am the light.
Deeply inhale through crown chakra, hold the breath, and say:
I am love.
Take a deep breath through the crown chakra, hold it, and say:
I am the creator of my life.
Move your fingers and open your eyes.

FINAL THOUGHTS

In this book, I have tried to give you the basics of Archangel Raziel's teachings.

I trust you got answers to your questions and this little guide was useful for you.

You can learn the secrets of the energy even more deeply if you use the highlighted messages in your meditation or think about them.

If you found the information interesting and would like to know about further manifestation teachings, please visit my website.

There, every Monday you will find another Weekly Manifestation Message (http://www.archangelwealthcoaching.com/weekly-manifestations) but you also have the opportunity to be a VIP member of the Angelic Wealth Club where you will continue to receive support for your wonderful and generous future. Weekly group messages, manifestation exercises, energy cleanings.

Since you bought the book, I would like to give you the first monthly membership gift.

You can join the FB group here. https://www.facebook.com/groups/214927279206423/

Try what Raziel Arkangyal taught you to create your dreams, be with us for 30 days and decide after that if you would like to continue.

If you prefer to create alone (as the co-creator of the Universe), you can take part in the Manifestation with Raziel Archangel online program.

http://www.archangelwealthcoaching.com/manifesting-with-archangel-raziel---online-program.html

The teachings continue.
The money subject we are working on is related to the creation of spiritual abundance.

The expected release date is January 2019.

Printed in Poland
by Amazon Fulfillment
Poland Sp. z o.o., Wrocław